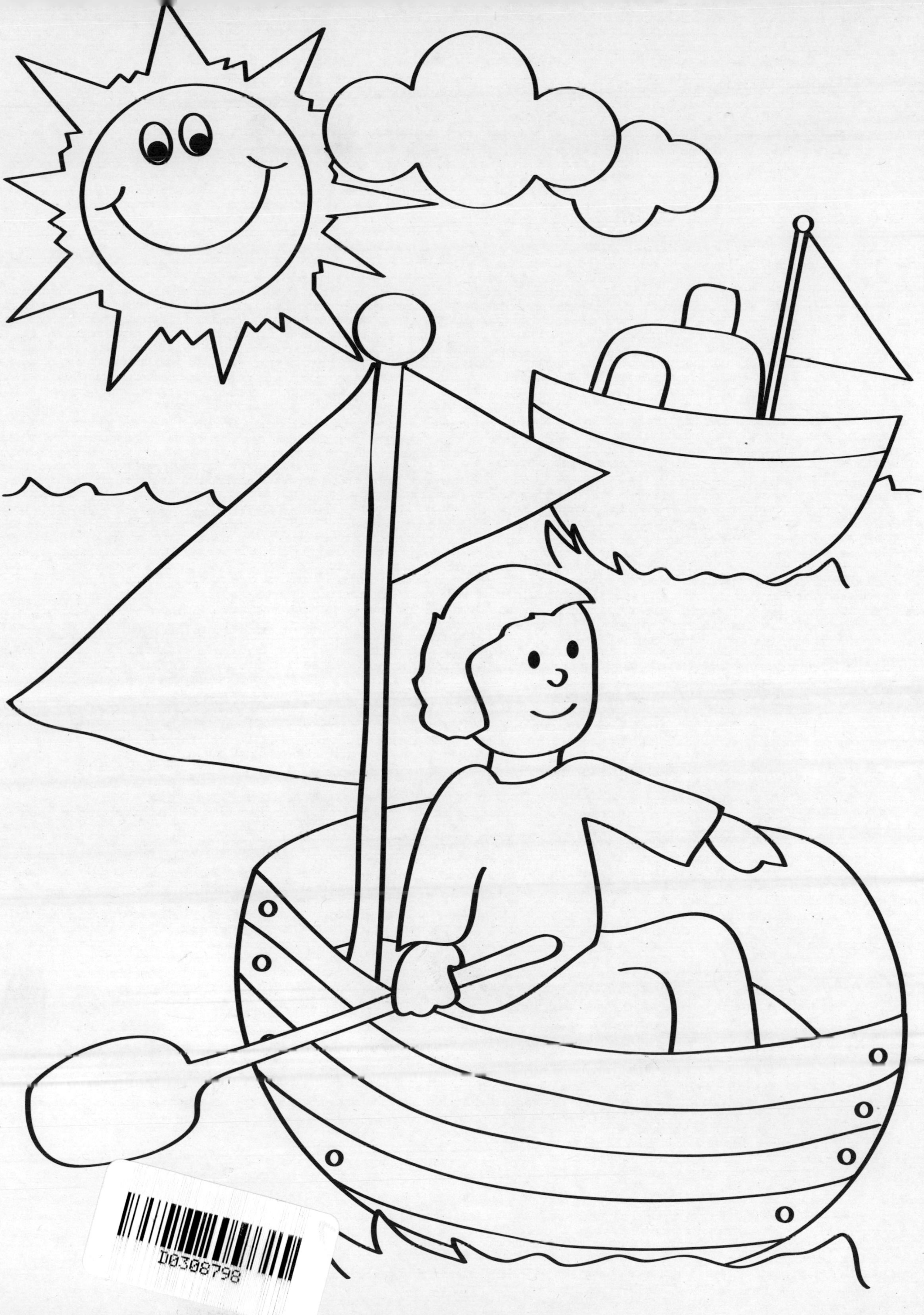

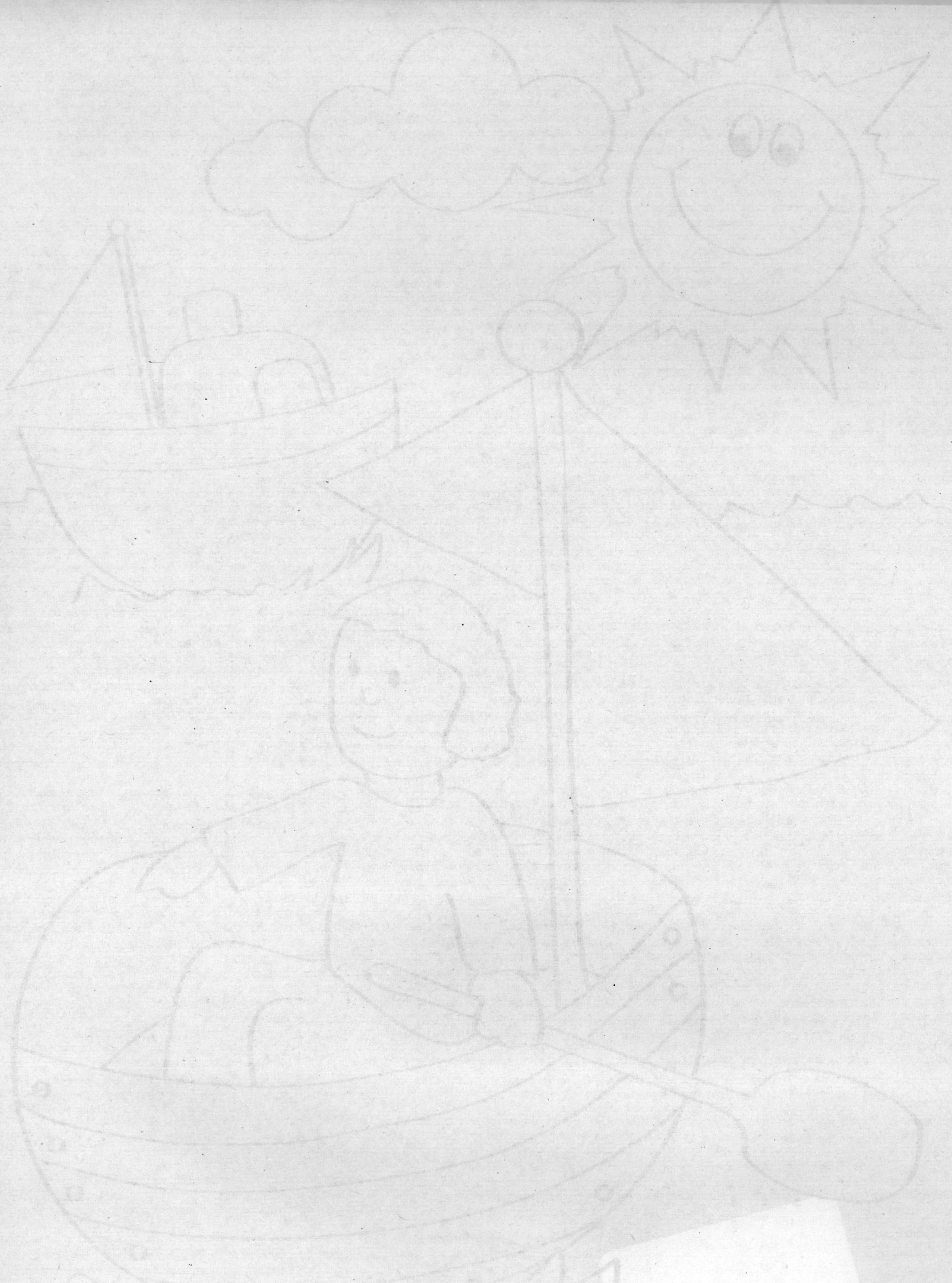

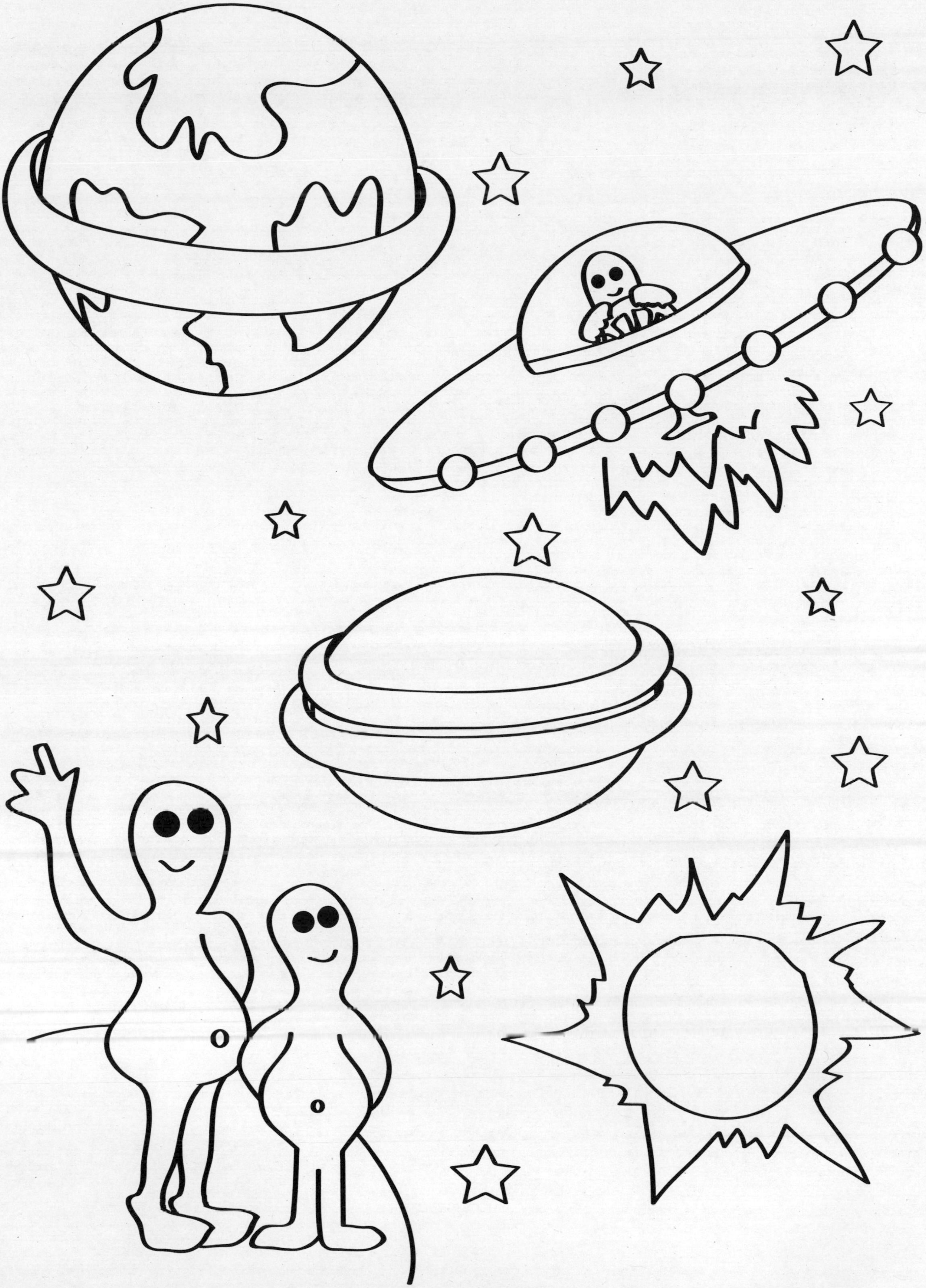

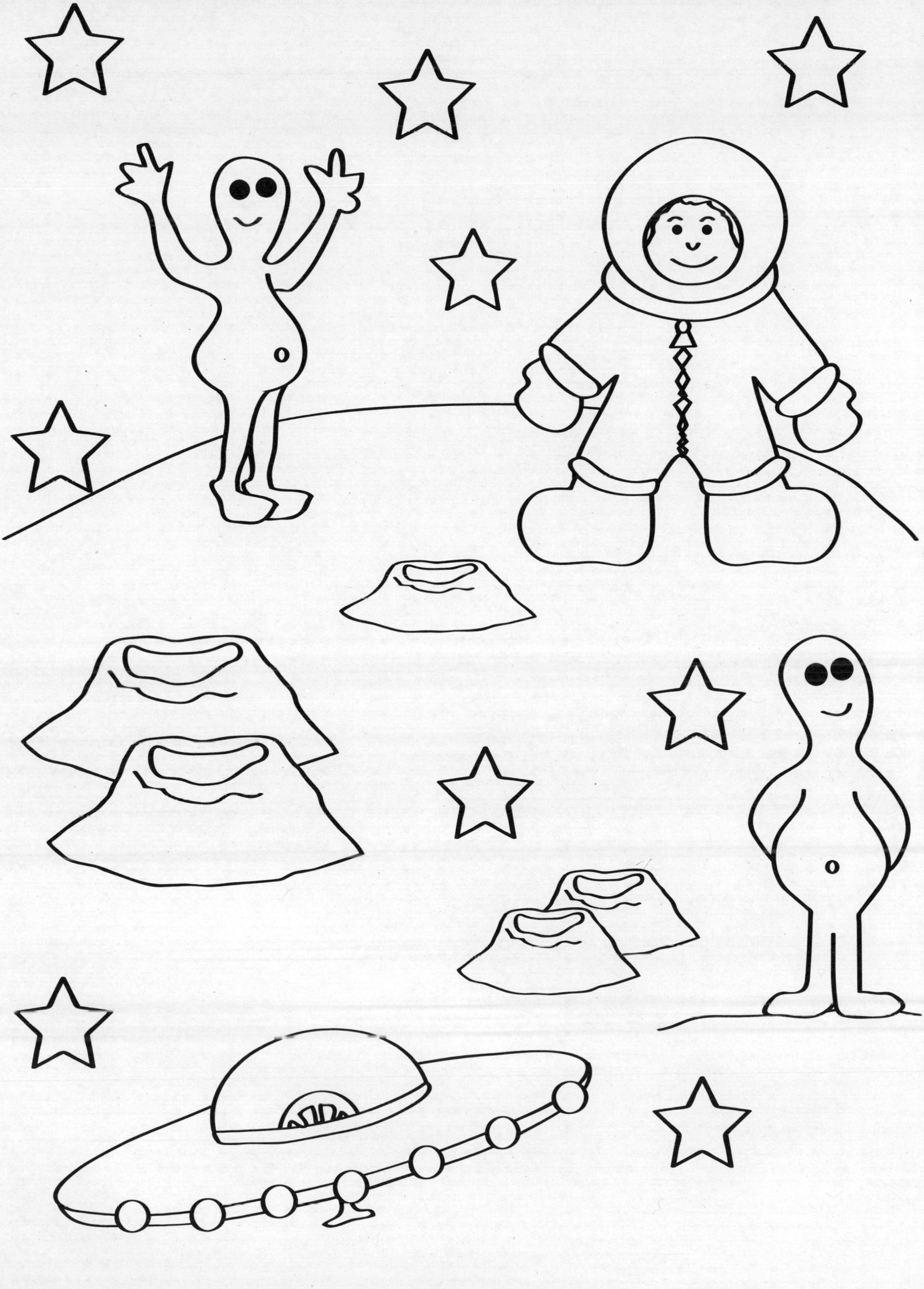

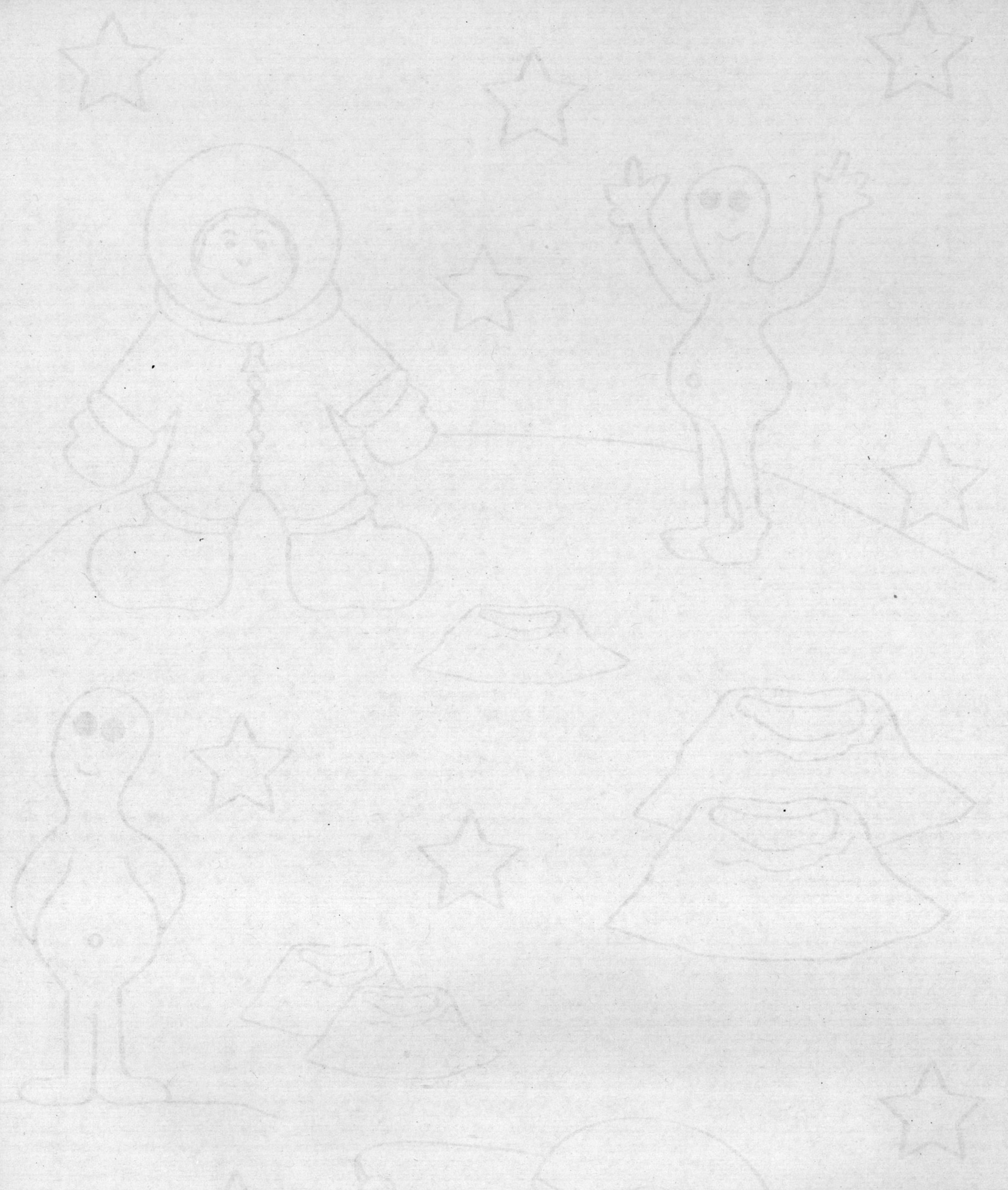

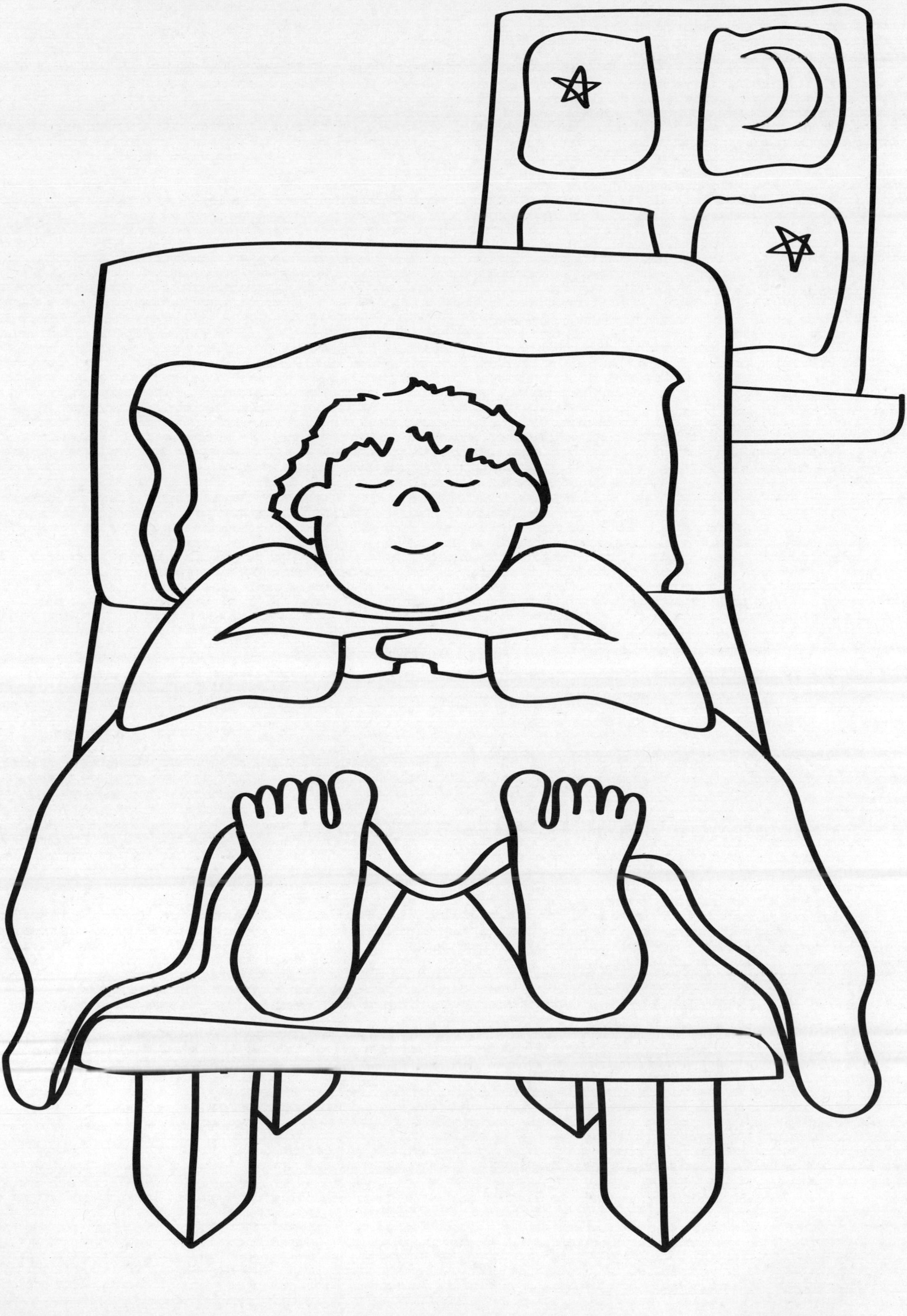

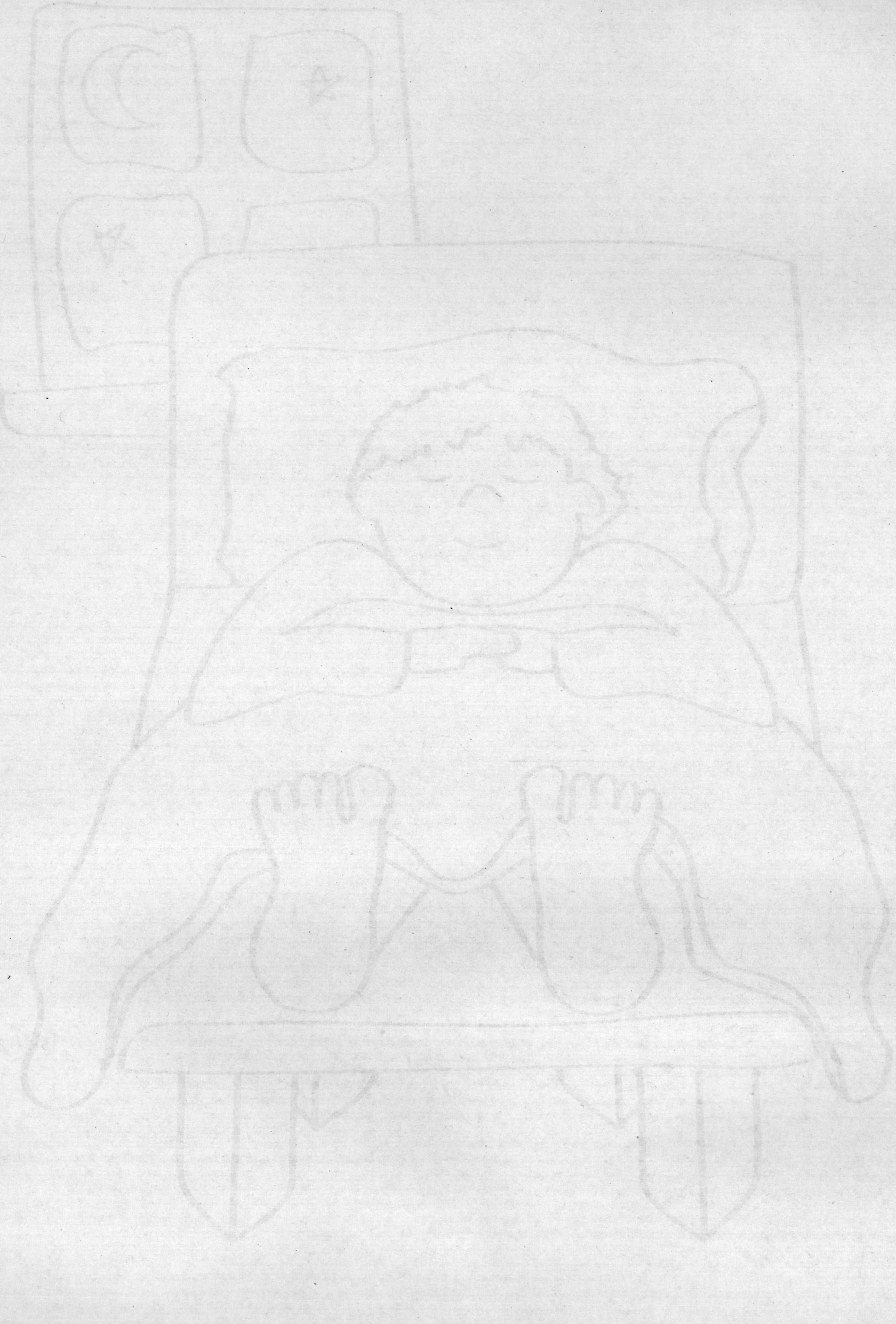

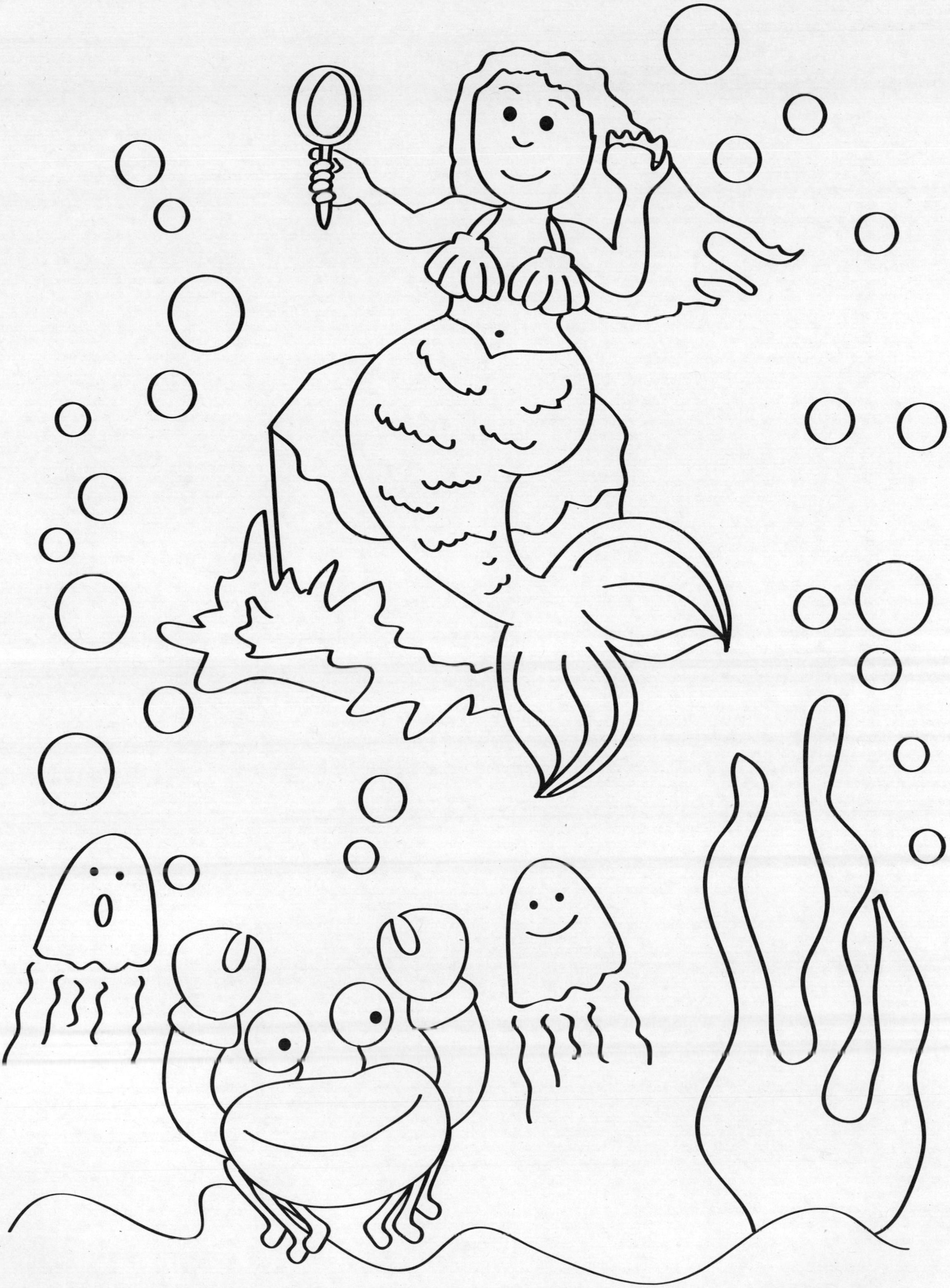

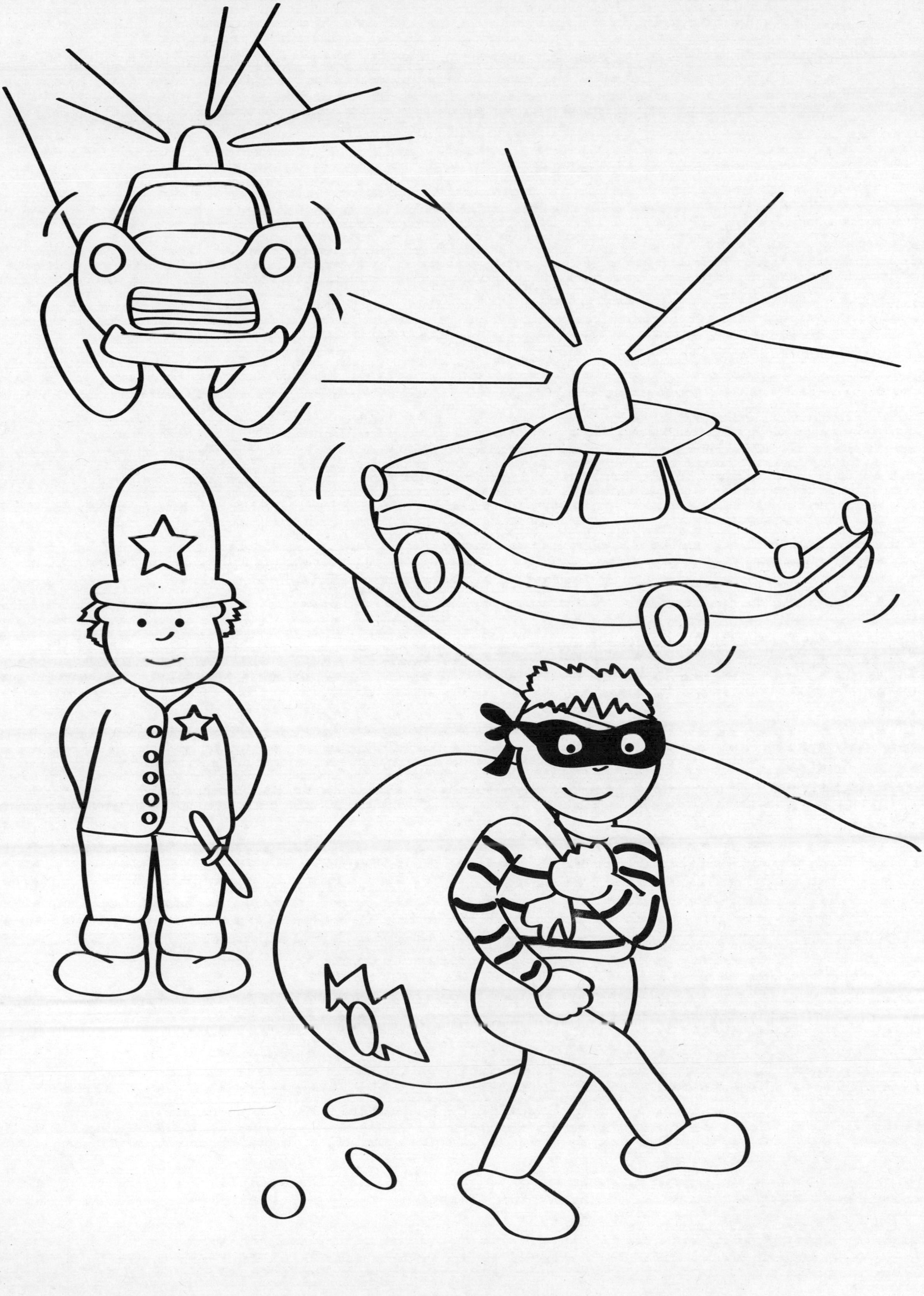

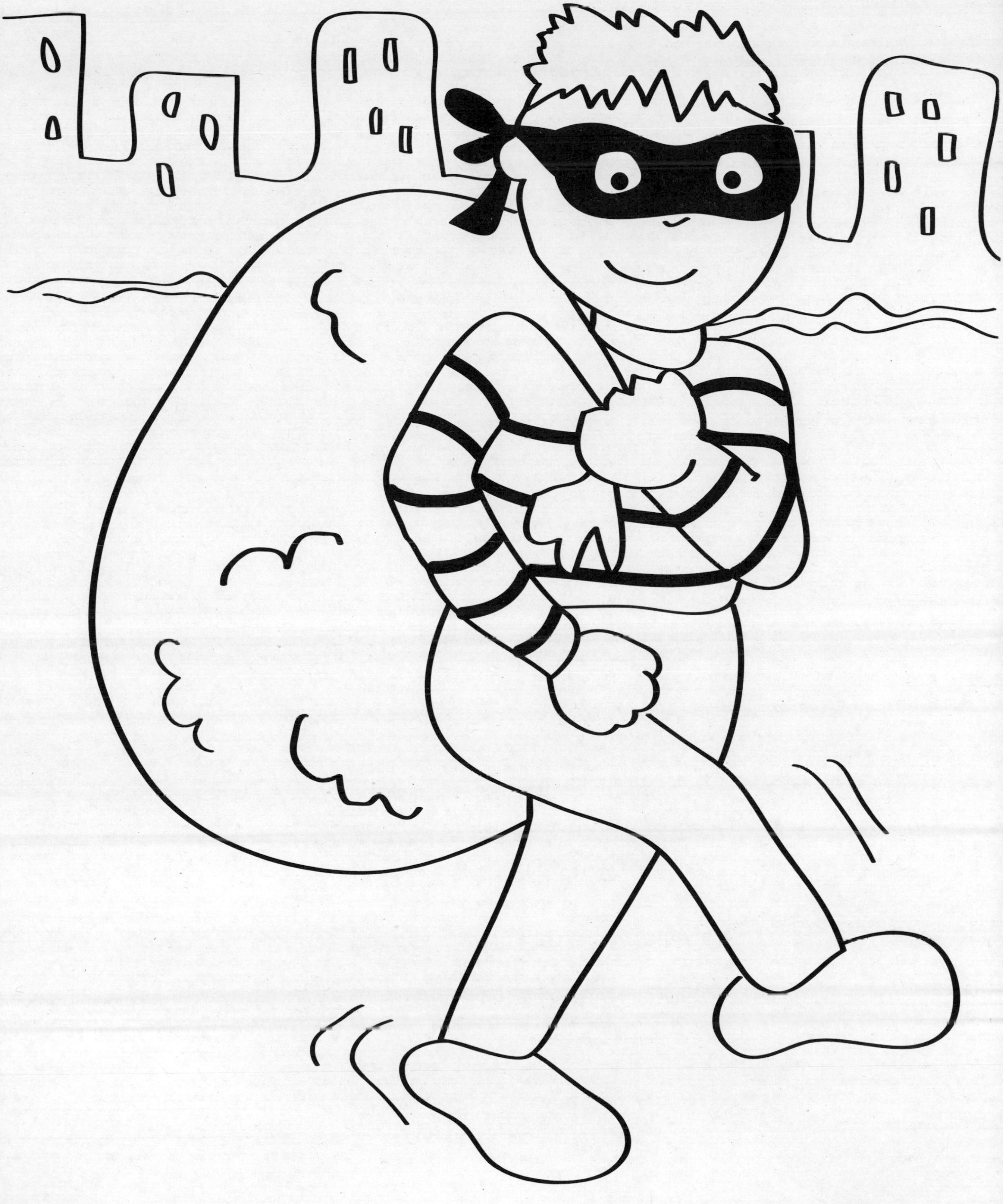

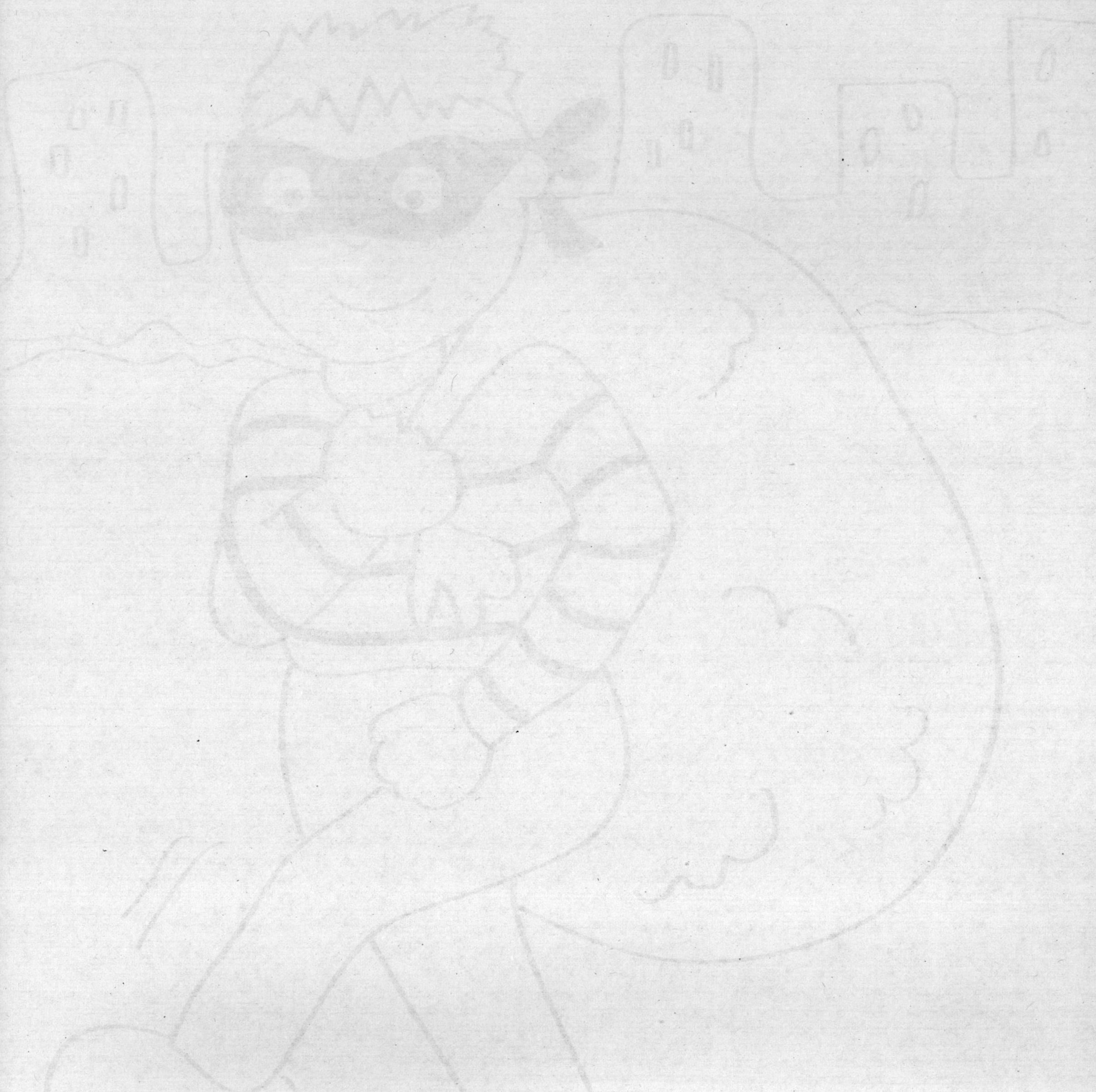

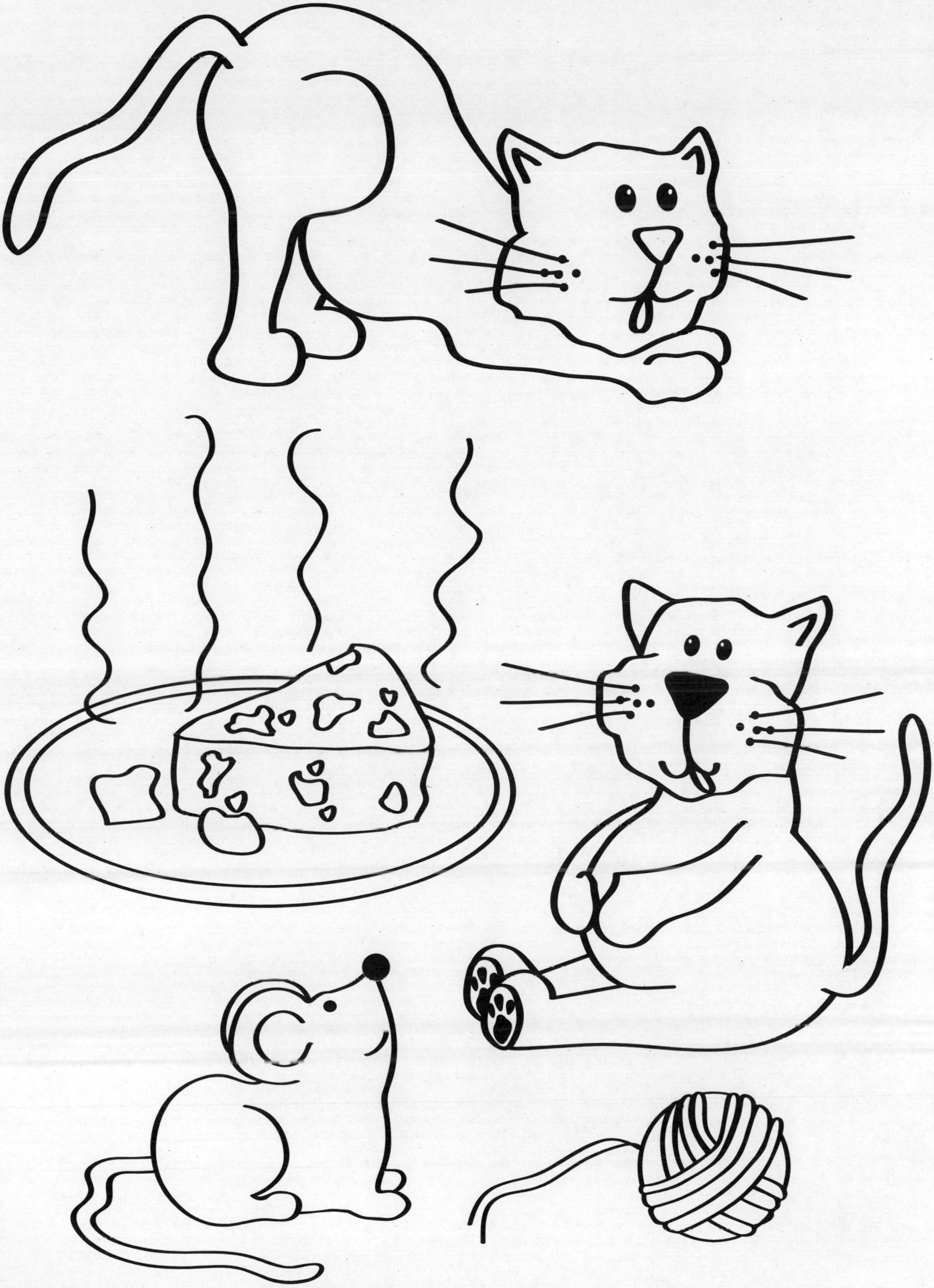

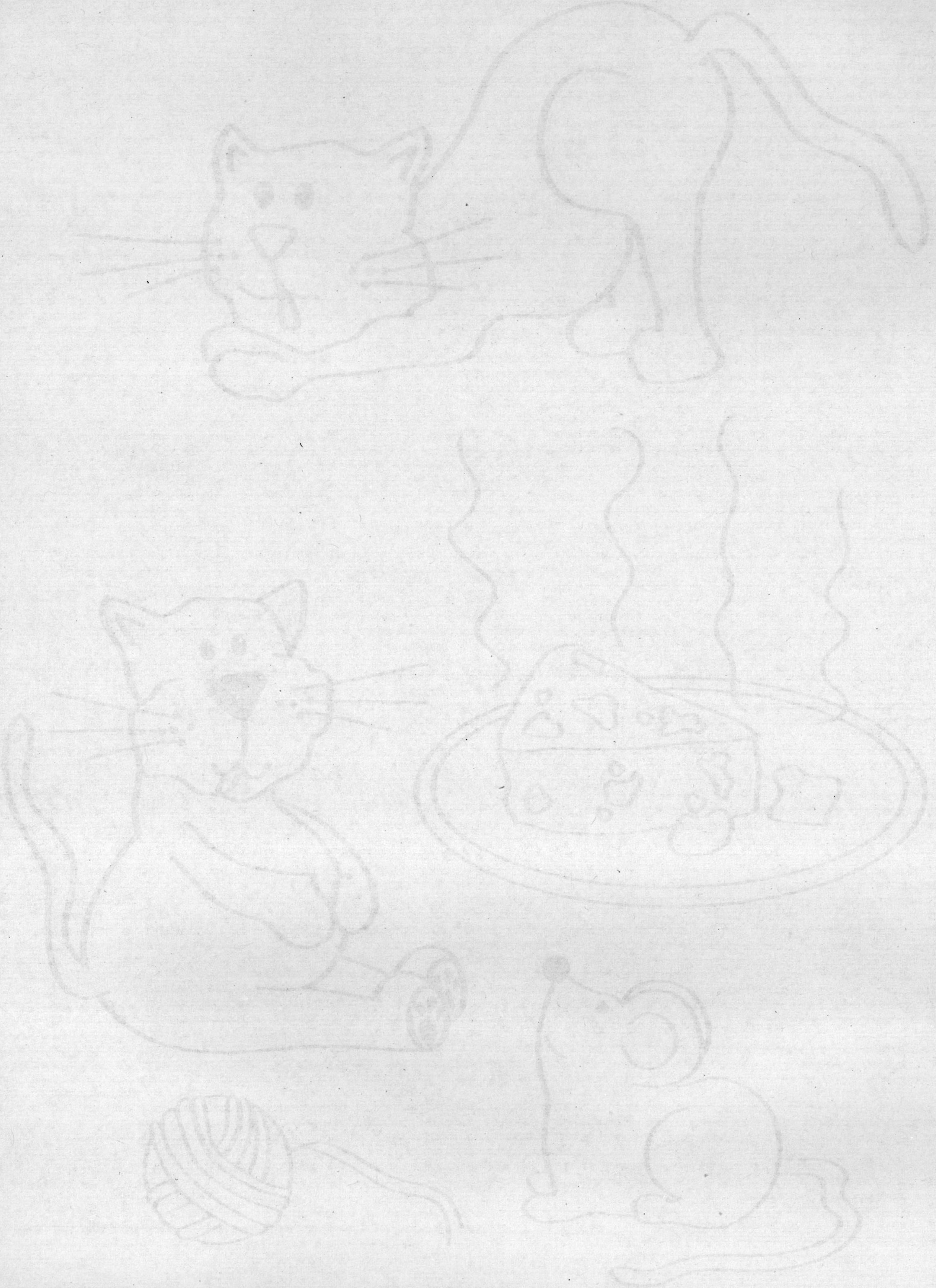

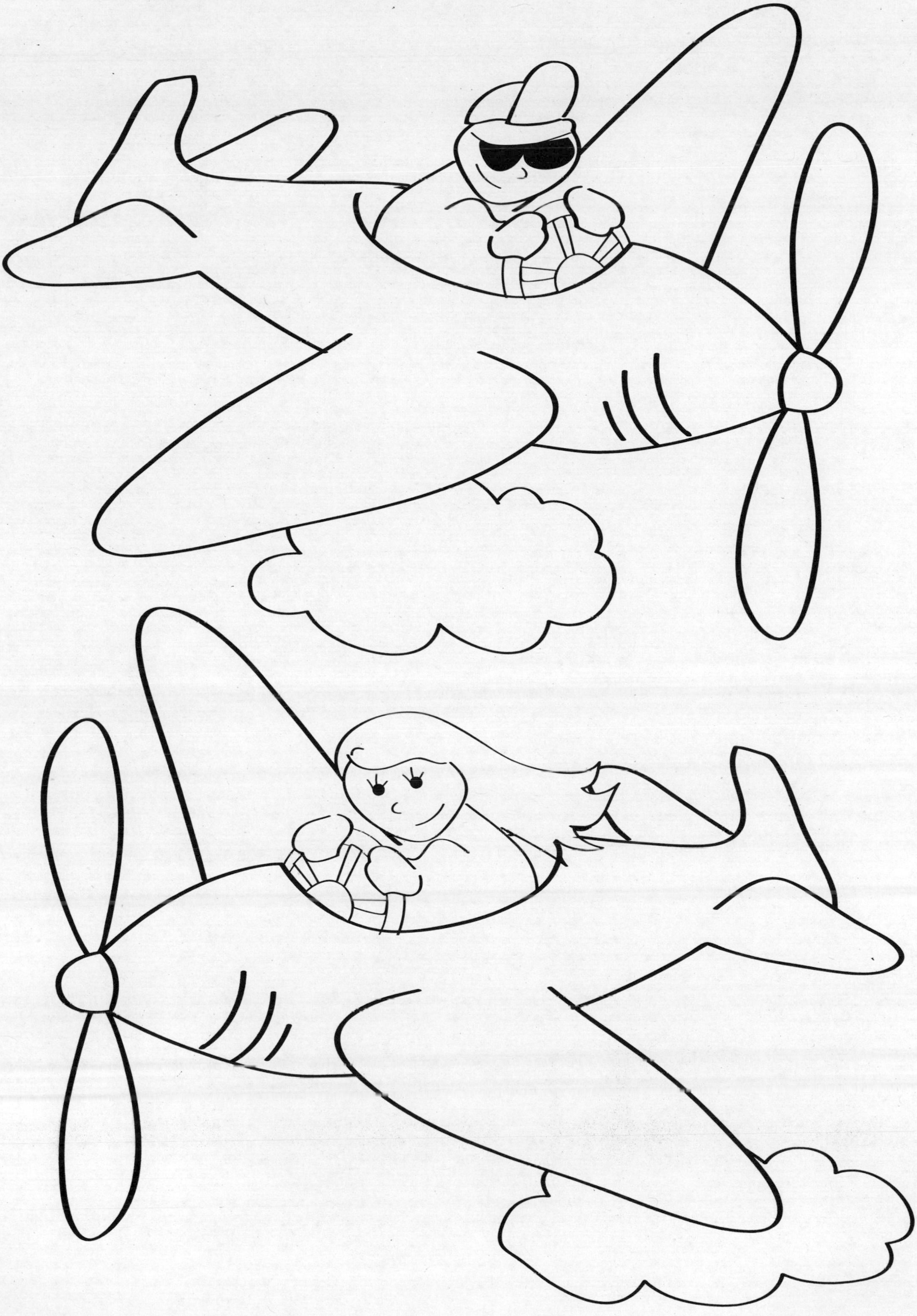

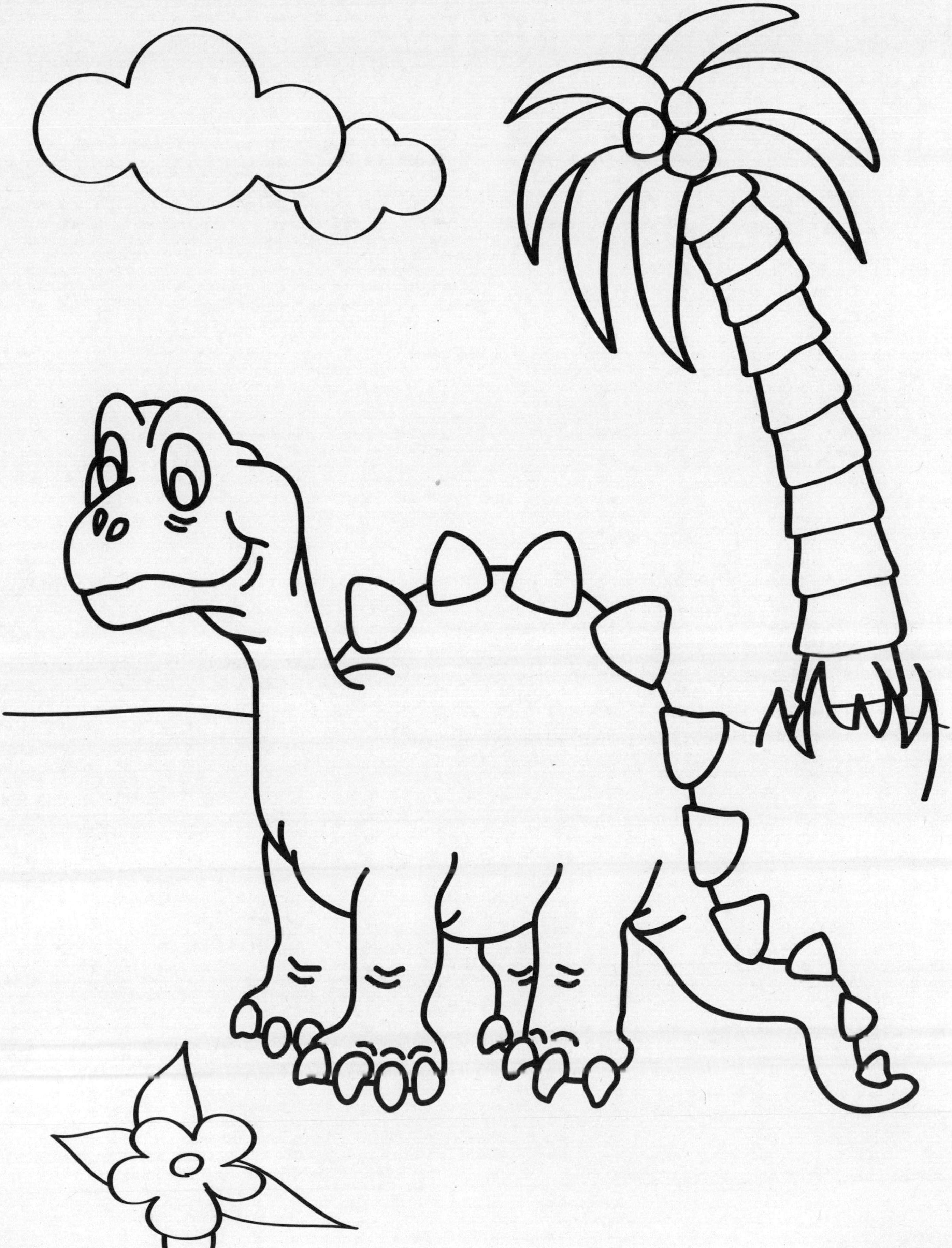

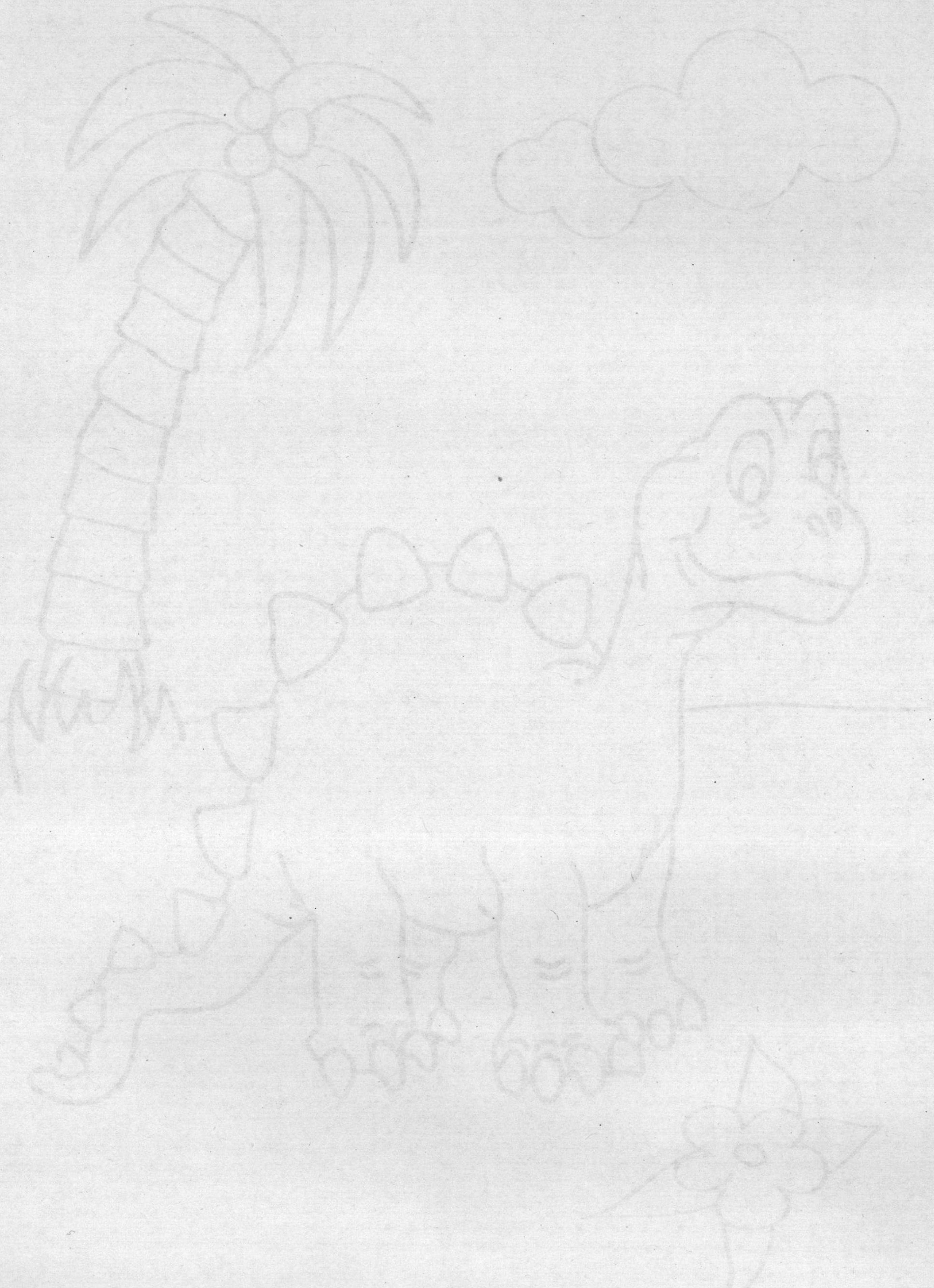

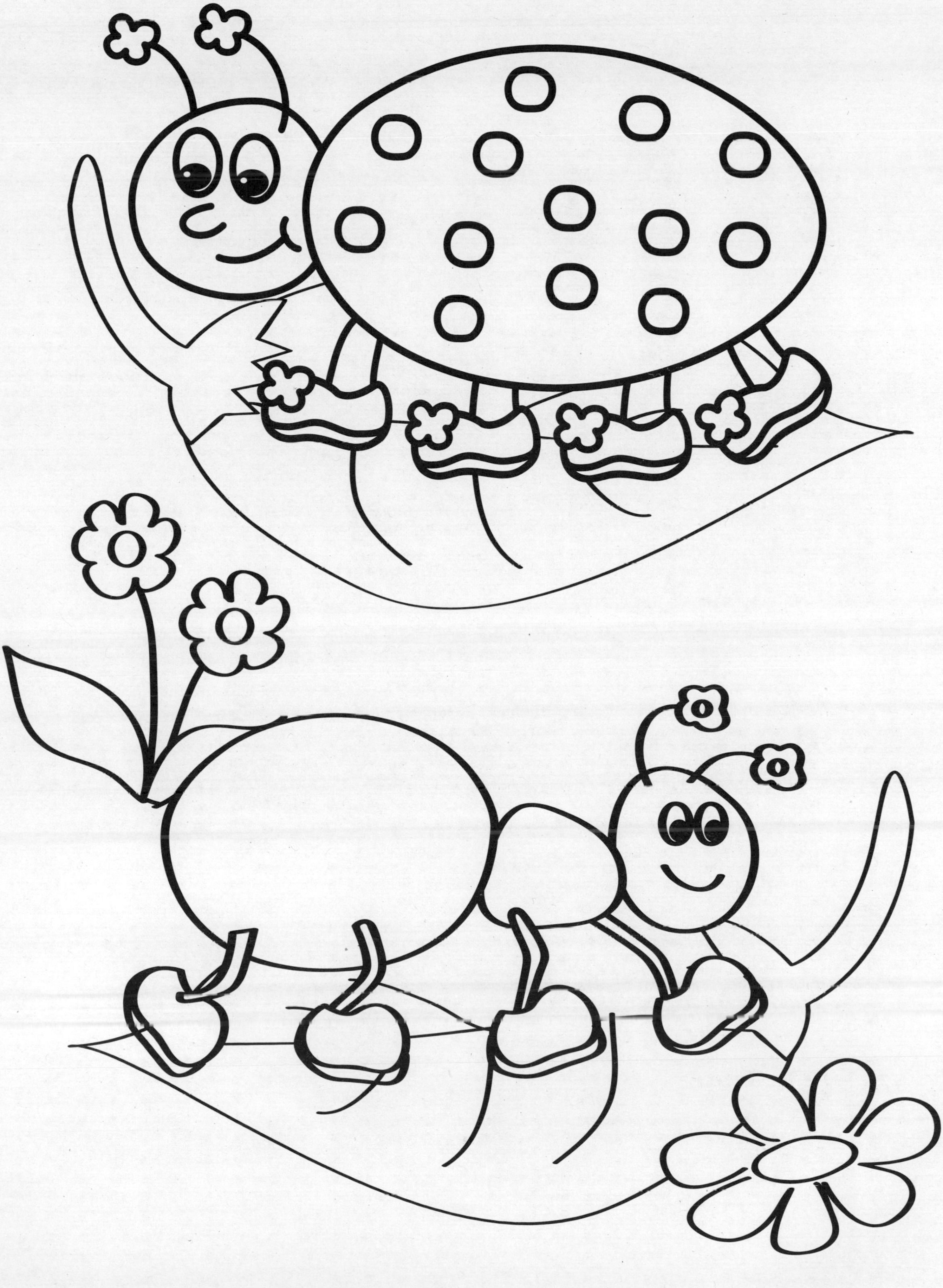

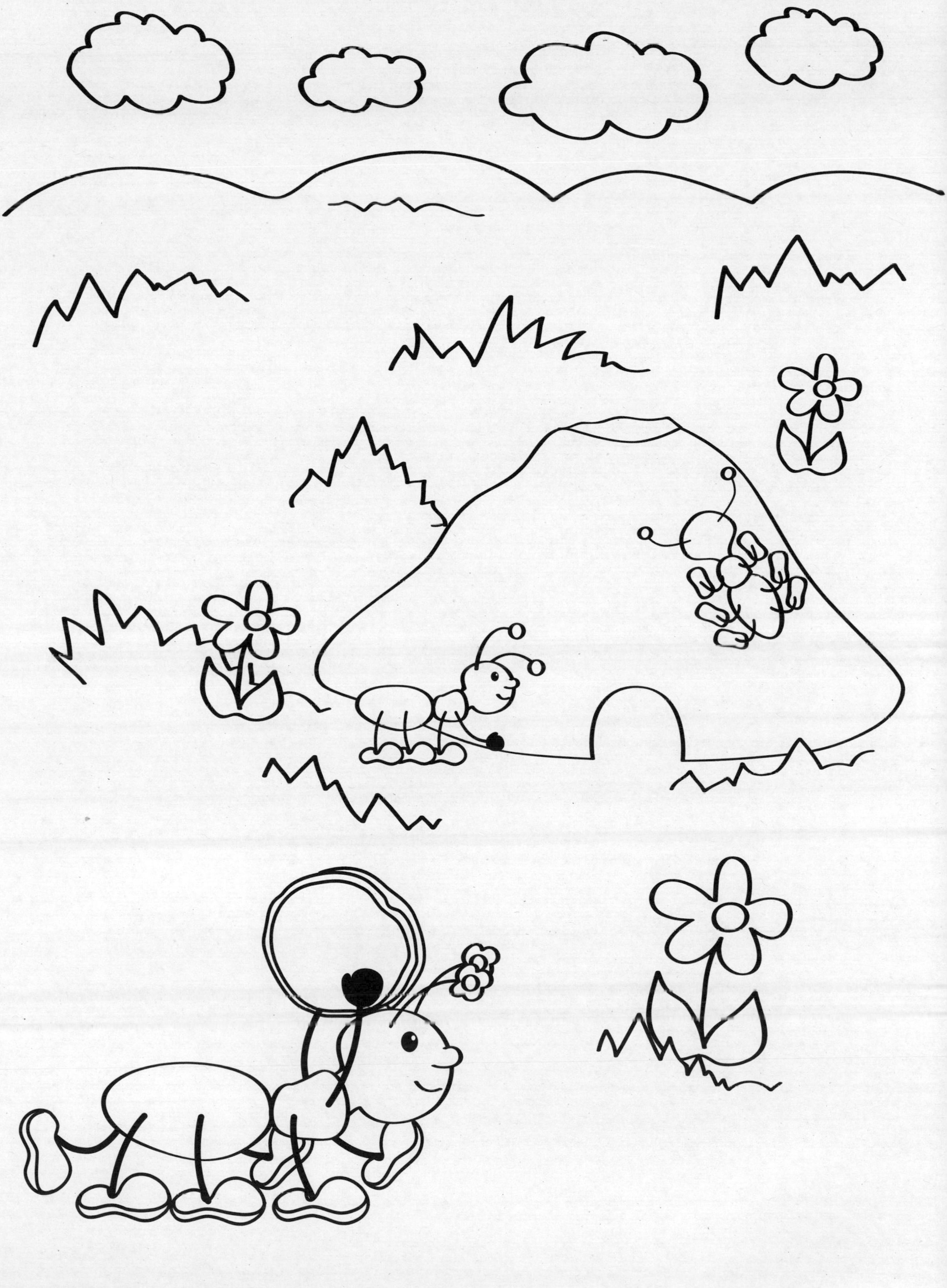

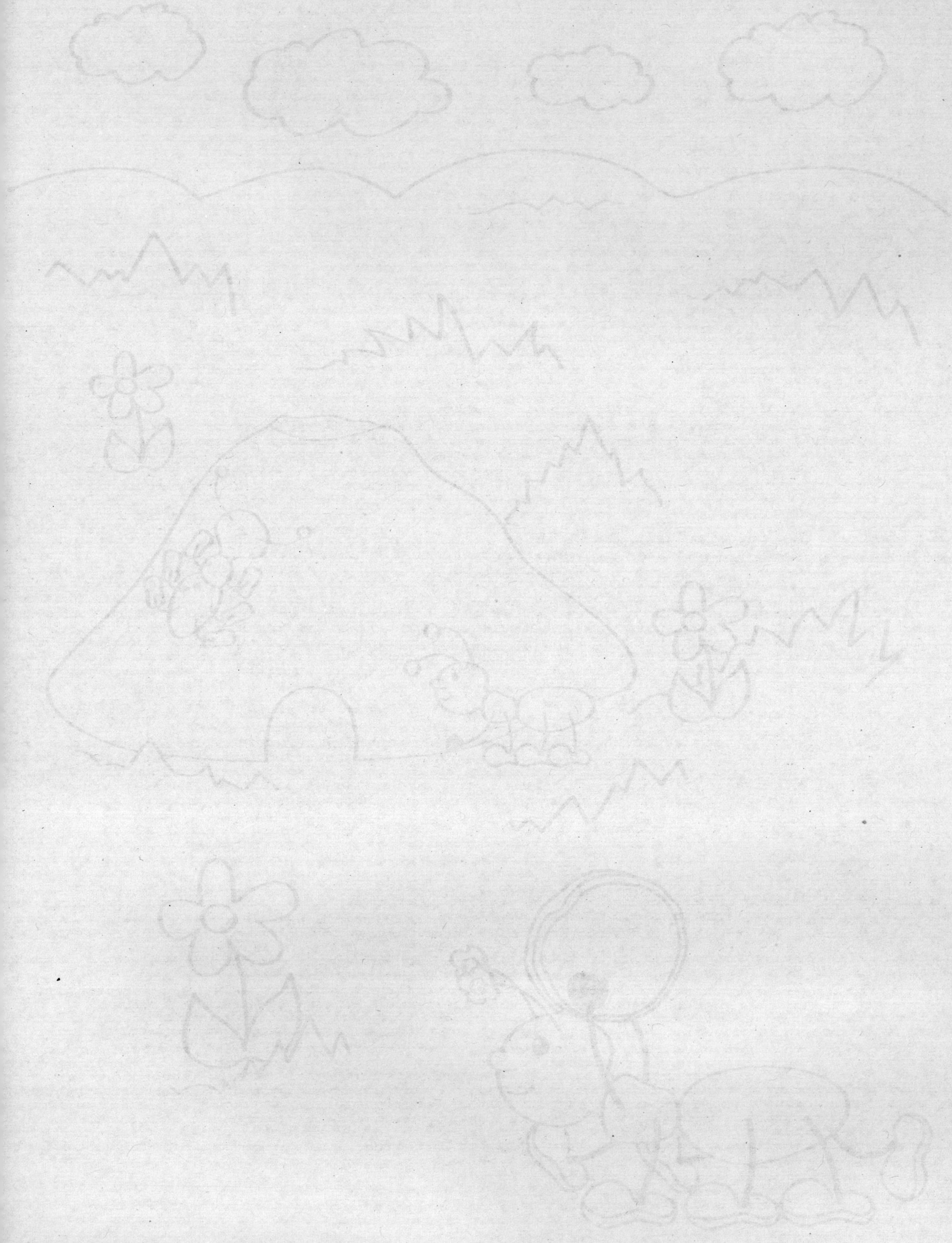

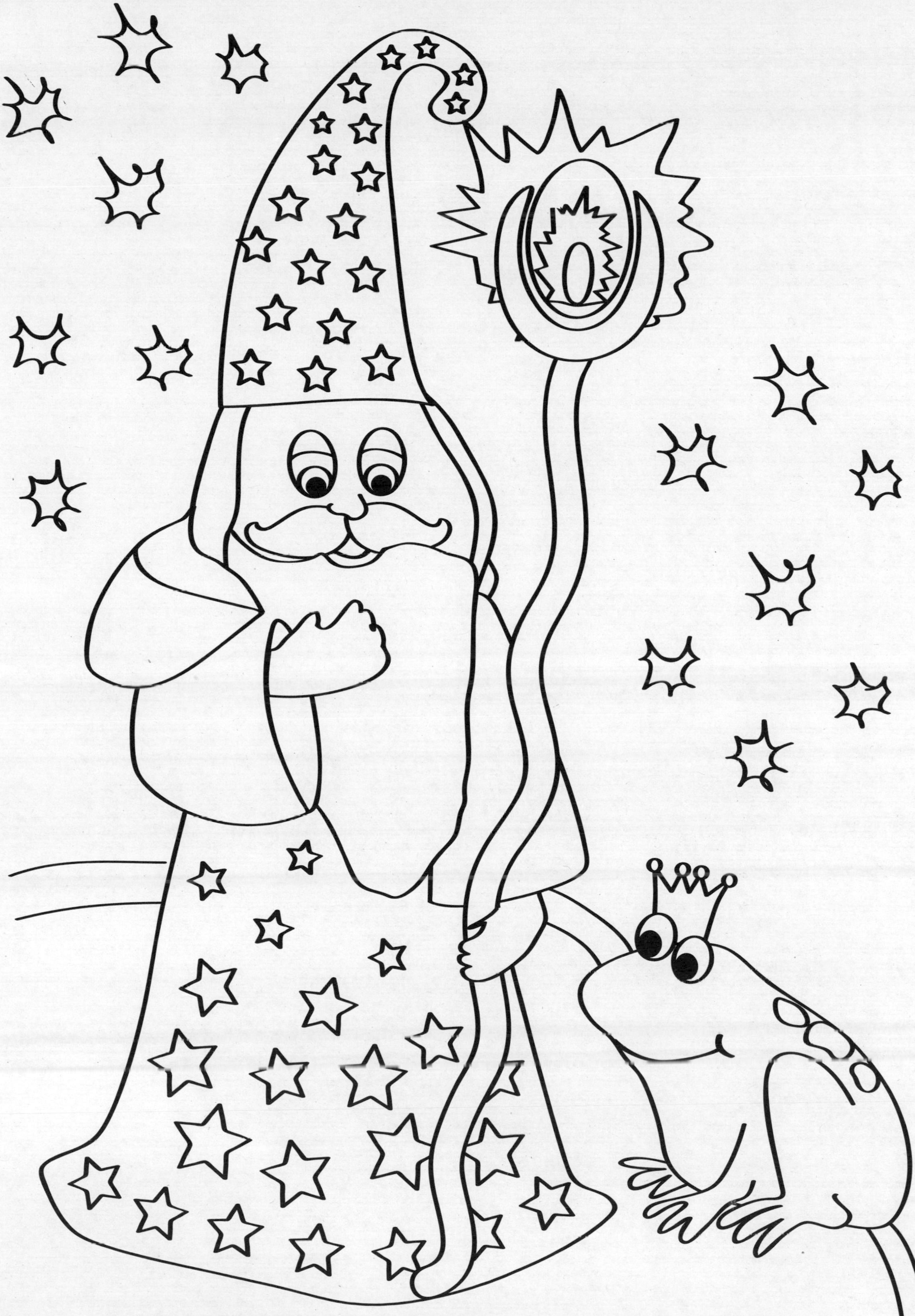

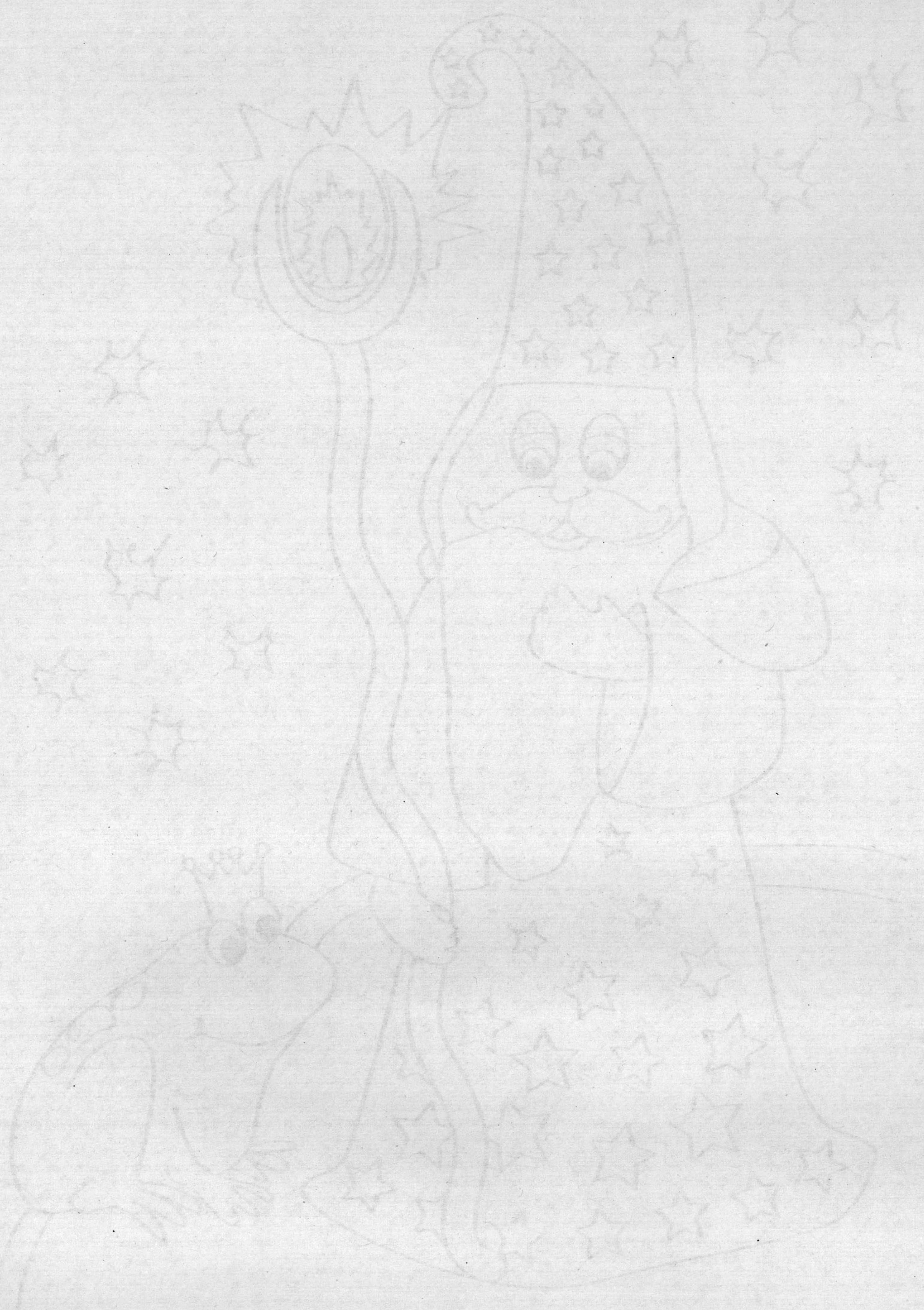

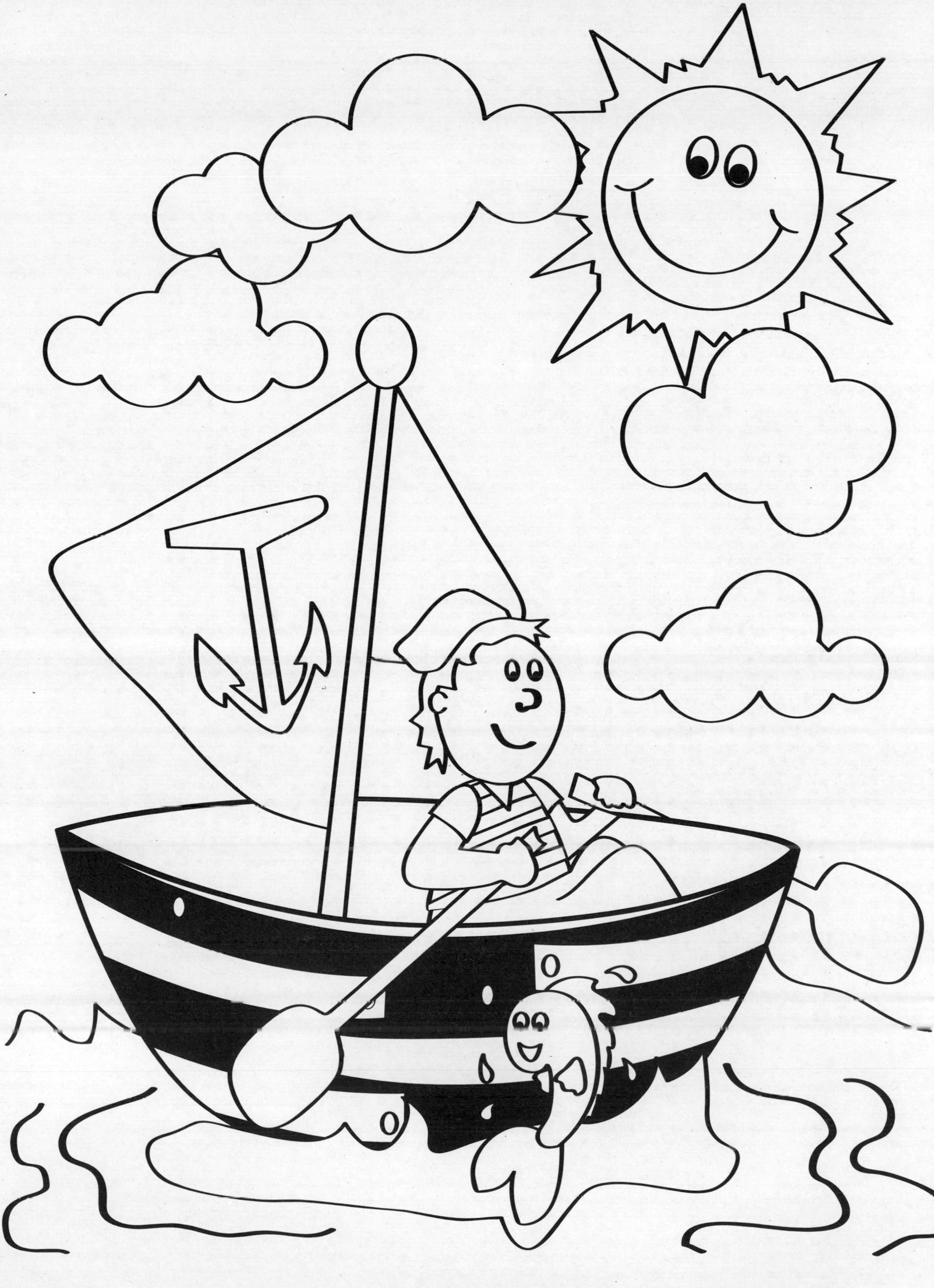

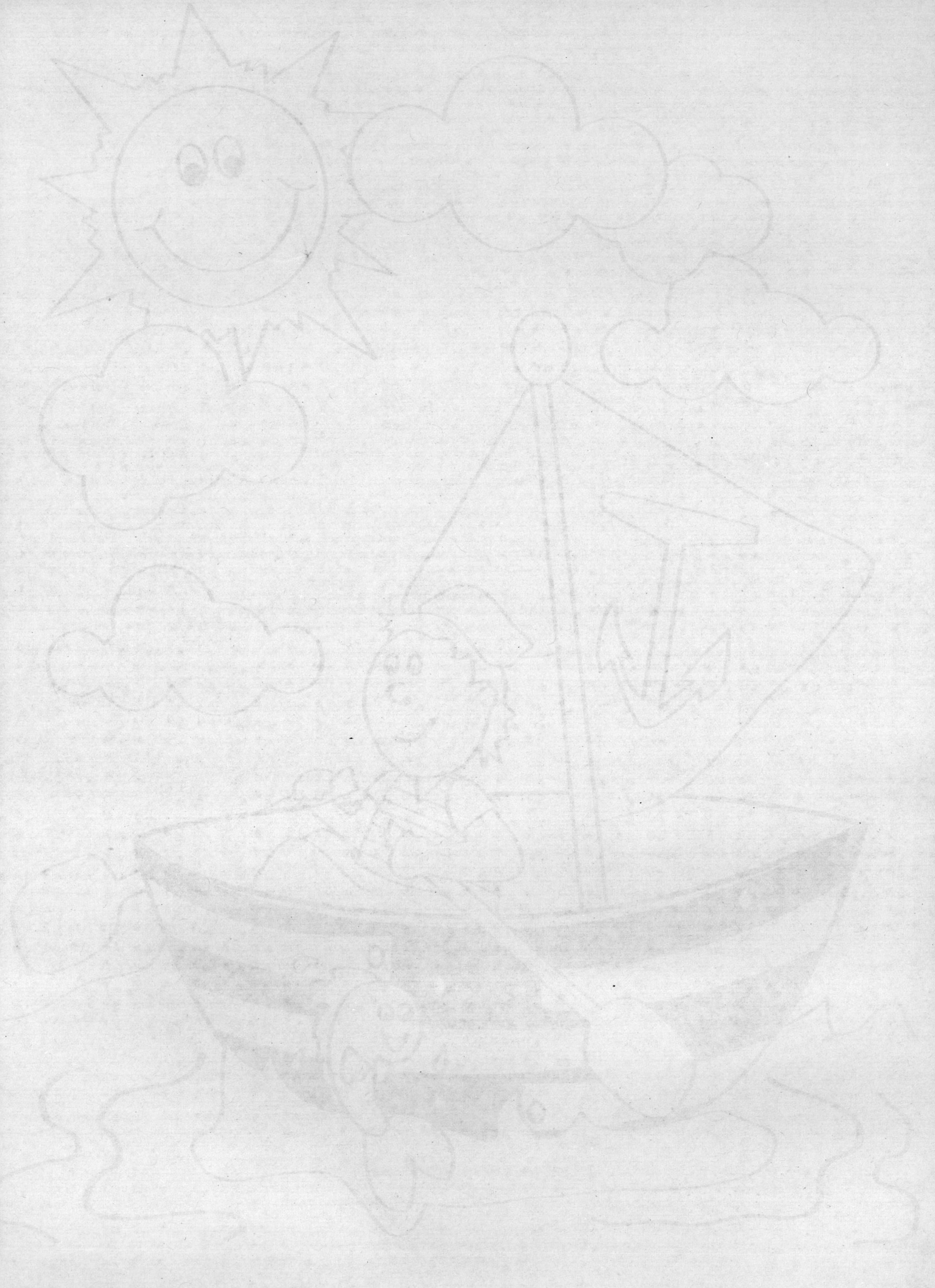

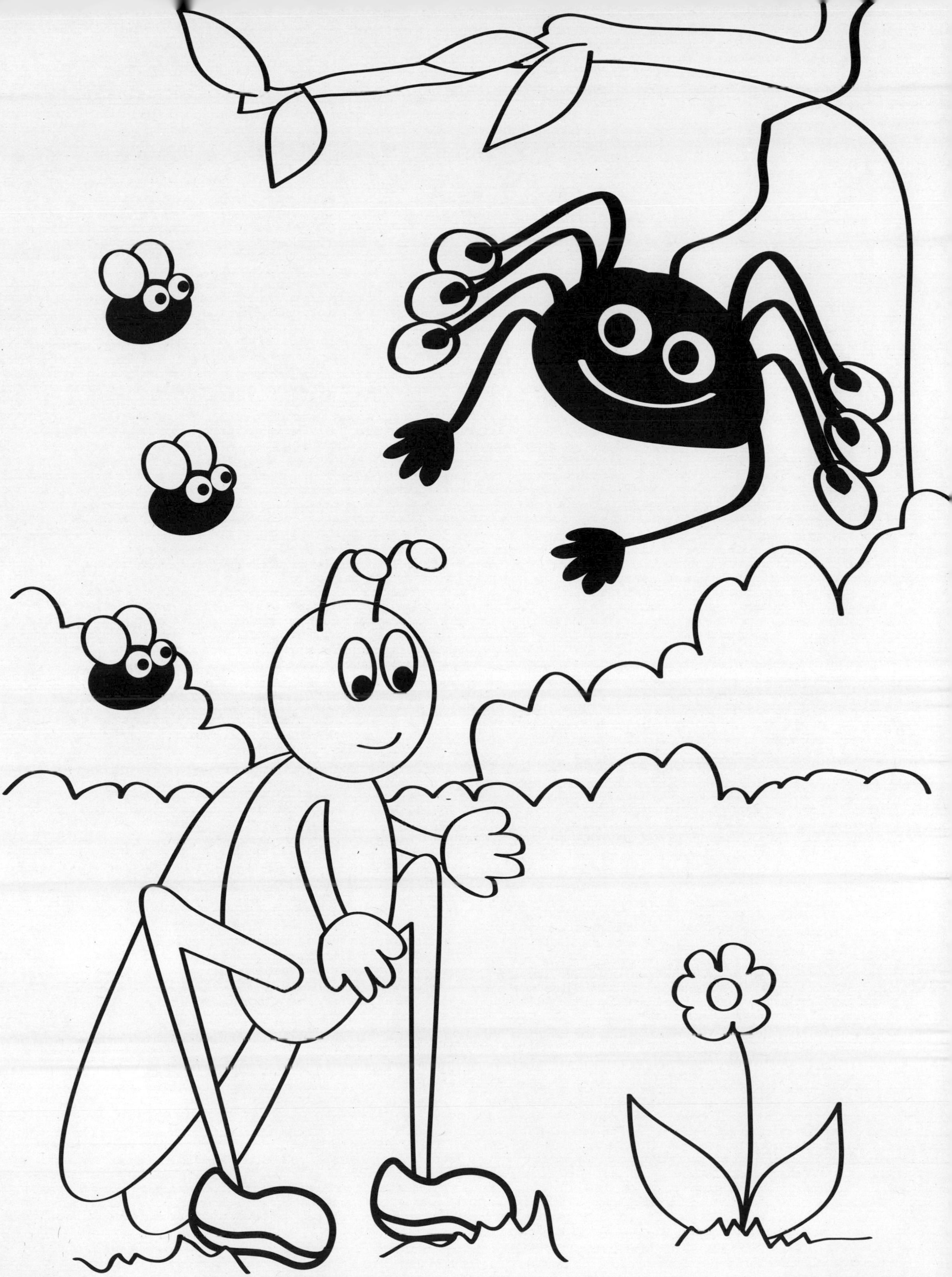

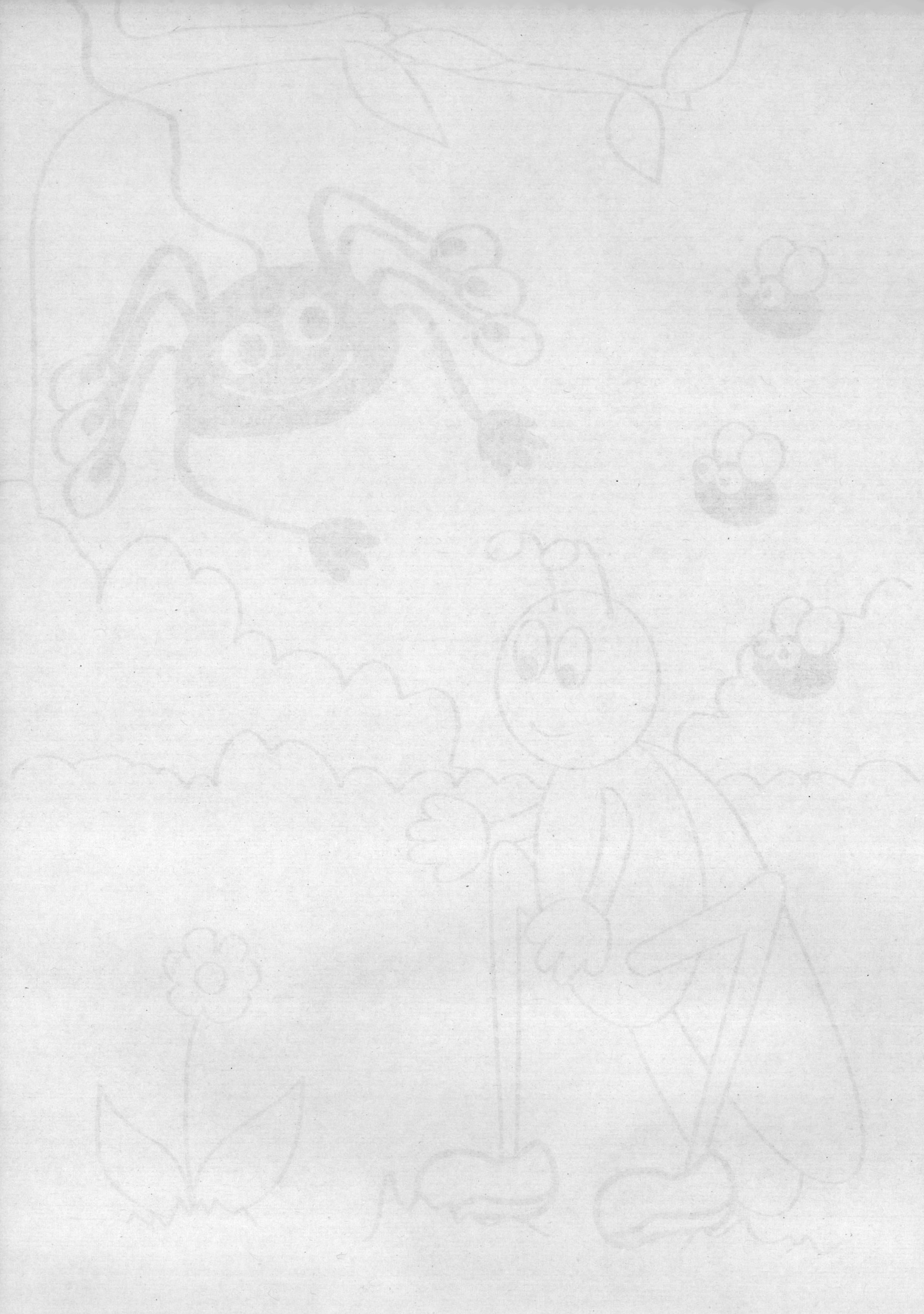

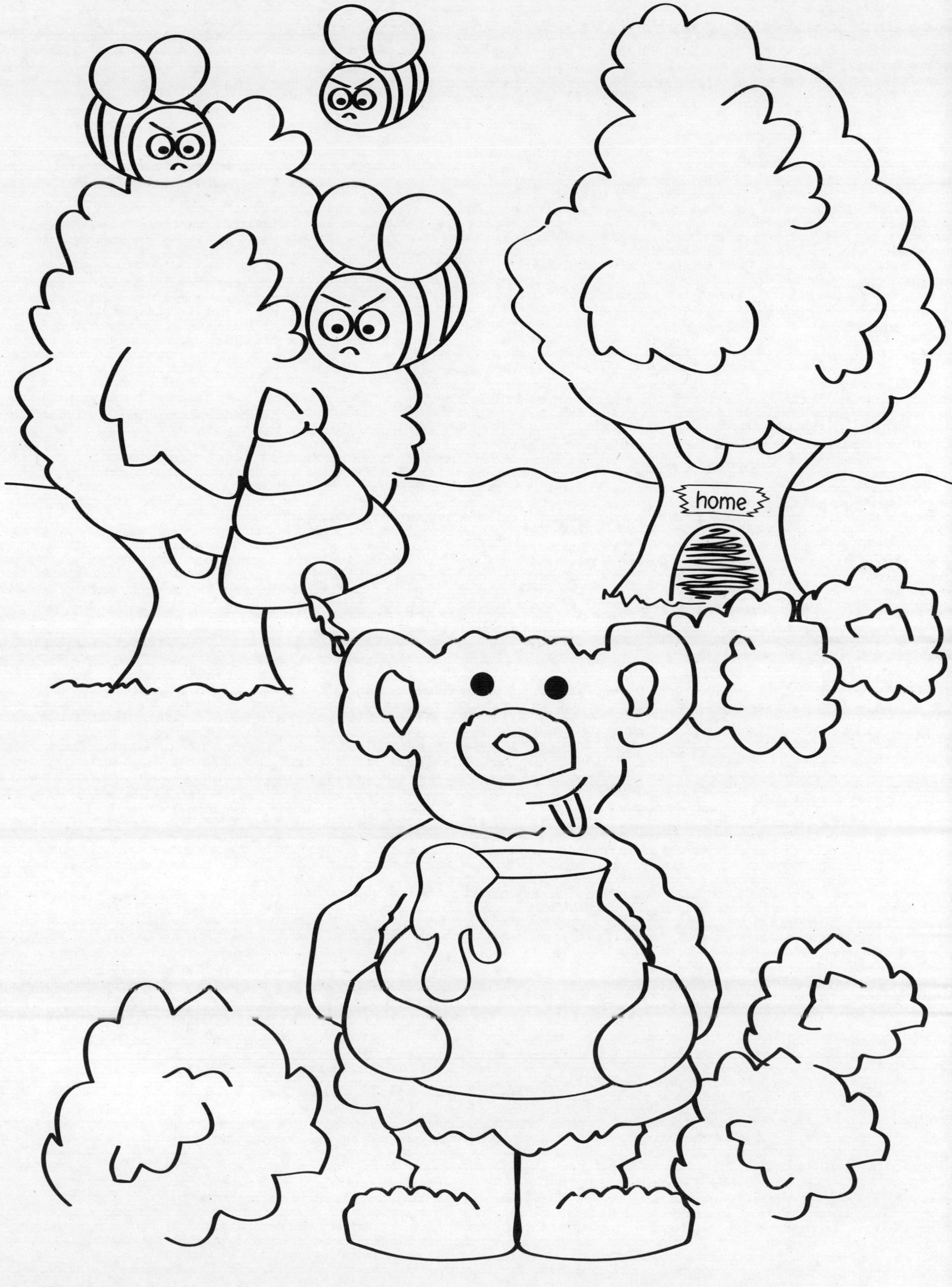
home

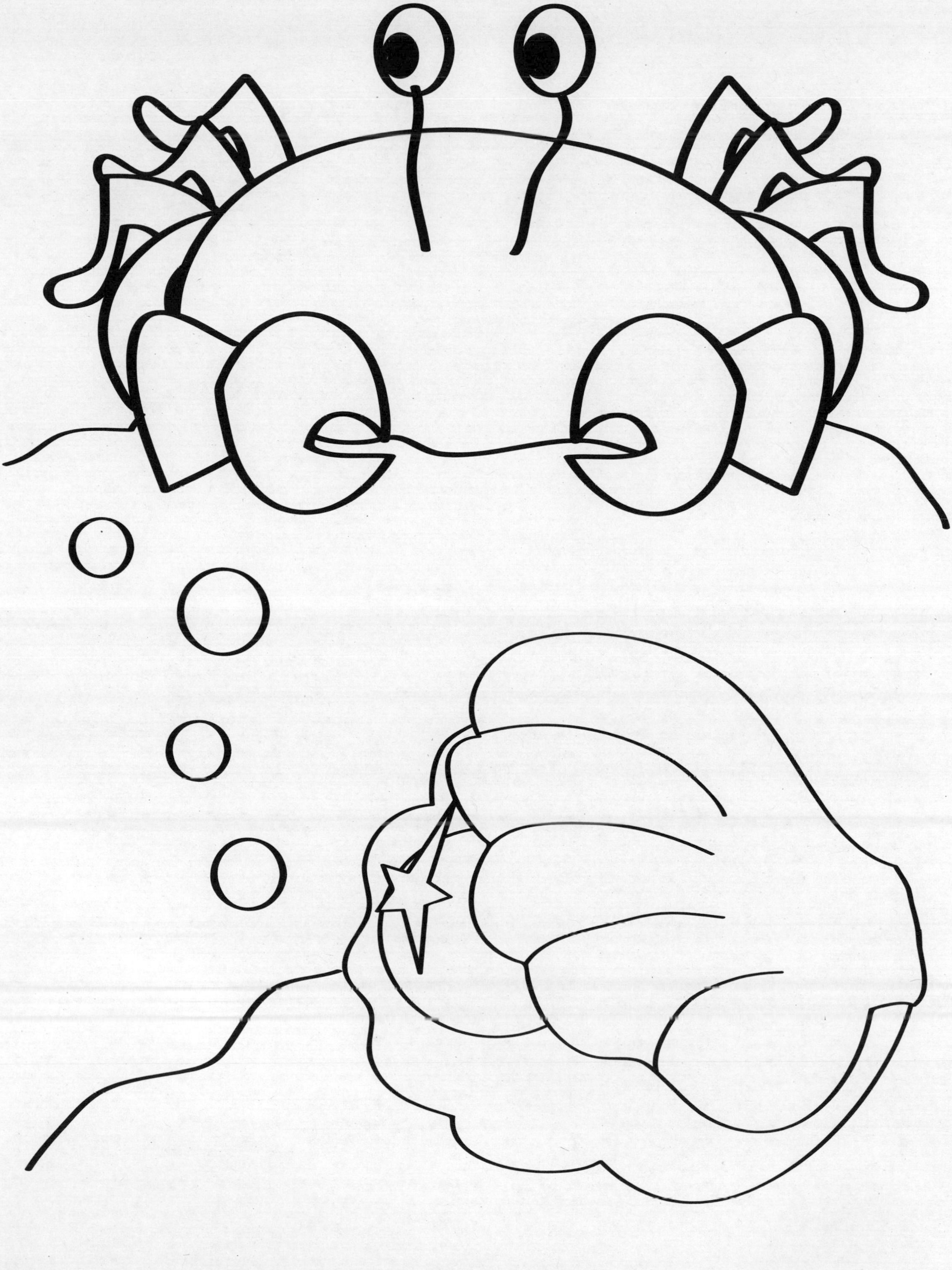

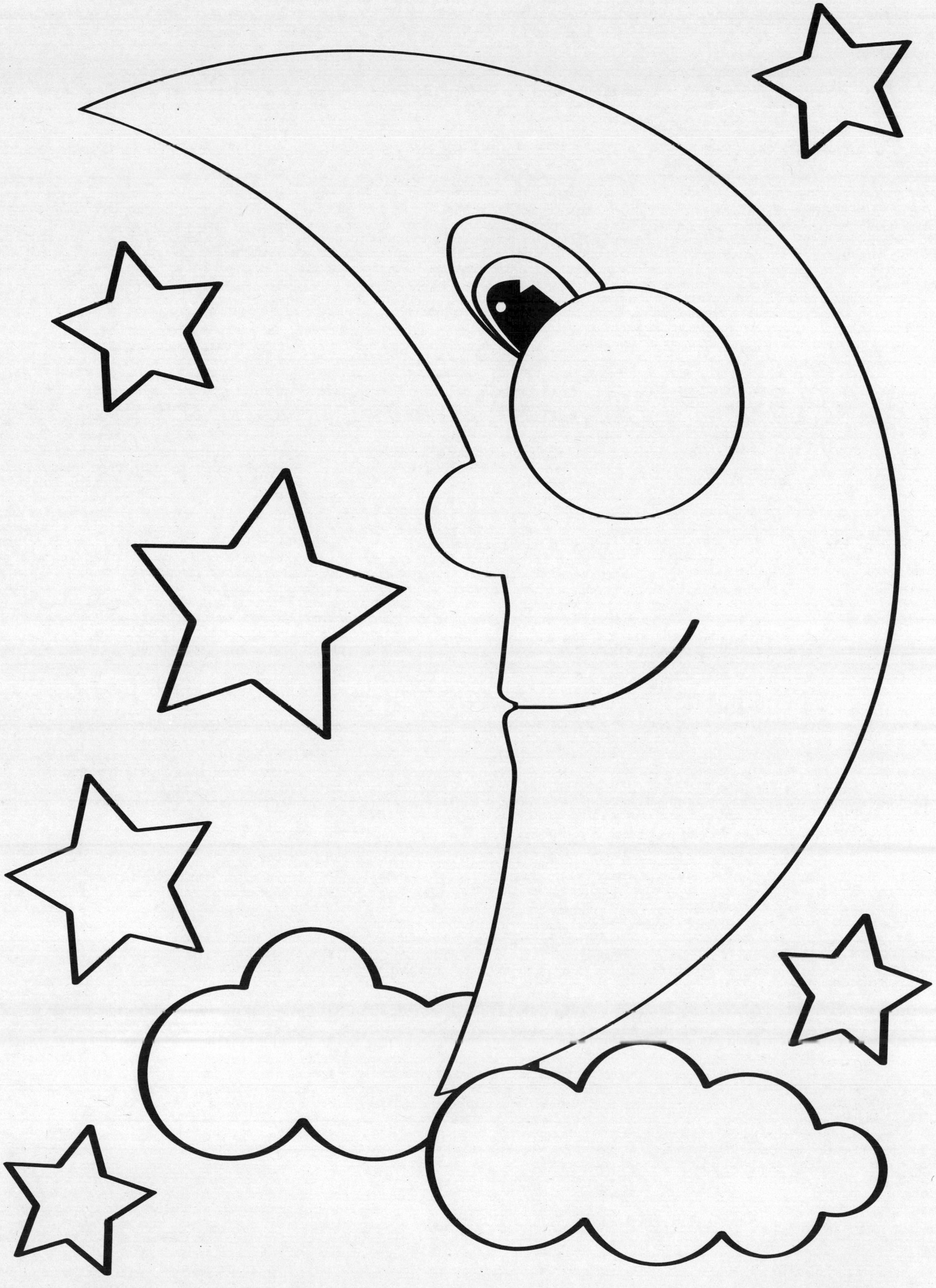

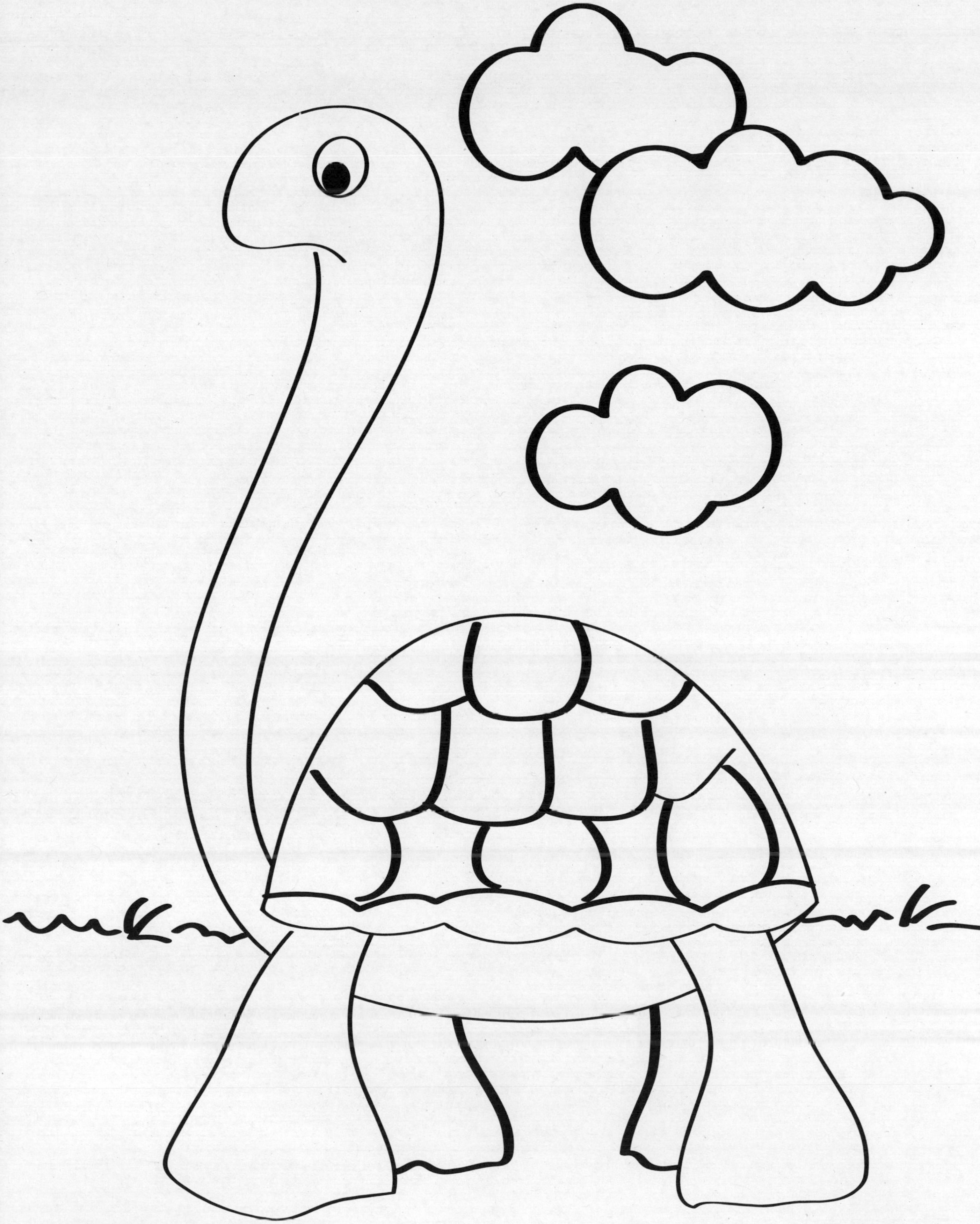

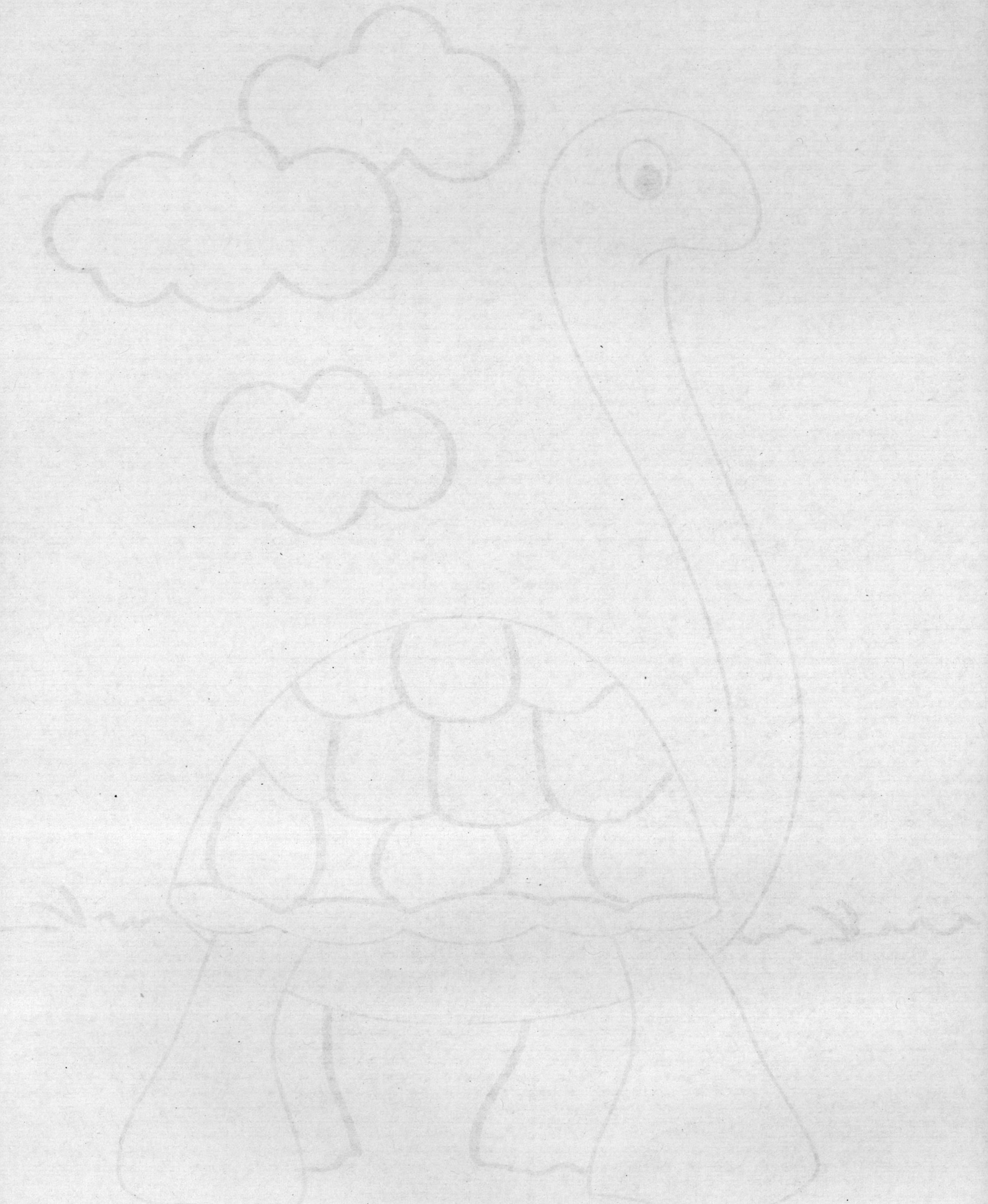